THE DICTIONARY OF
SOC·CER

THE DICTIONARY OF
soc·cer

WRITTEN BY RICK BRAITHWAITE
ILLUSTRATED BY MATT MYERS

COOL CHANGE PUBLISHING *PORTLAND, OREGON*

Library of Congress Cataloging-in-Publication Data.

Braithwaite, Rick.
    The dictionary of soccer/written by Rick Braithwaite; illustrated by Matt Myers.
        p.   cm.
Summary: Presents humorous definitions of soccer terms arranged in alphabetical order.
ISBN 0-940893-02-9: $5.95
1. Soccer—Humor. [1. Soccer—Dictionaries. 2. Soccer—Wit and humor.] I. Myers, Matt, ill. II. Title.
PN6231.S632B7 1989
796.334'0207—dc20   89-9796
                                      CIP

796.334
B 814 d

Printed in the United States of America.

Cover and book design: Tom Kelly

Published by Cool Change Publishing
P.O. Box 40426
Portland, Oregon 97240-0426

Current Printing

10 9 8 7 6 5 4 3 2

Dedicated to the memory of
Peter Evan Smith
1934-1986

a **able-bodied:** one of two conditions required to play, coach, or referee a soccer game (see *dim-witted*).

absent: the only condition a soccer player can be in to avoid making mistakes and escape getting injured. Also a useful means of avoiding having to share plastic water bottles with sweaty teammates.

ace bandage: elastic strap used to strengthen ankles, provide padding for sore muscles, and tie nets to goalposts when the assistant coach forgot to bring the shower hooks.

achilles tendon: strongest and longest tendon in the body, this important rubber-like strap has no discernible use in soccer except to be blamed for slowness ("It's tight"), lack of agility ("It's loose"), inability to kick the ball for any distance ("It's sore"), unwillingness to pass ("It's bruised"), and unwillingness to carry net bags back to the parking lot (all of the above).

adult soccer: any soccer game whose participants are older than they act (see *youth soccer*).

advantage: getting the upper hand on a competitor by controlling the ball, retaining possession of the ball, or marrying the referee's sister or brother.

aggressive: a popular mode of play characterized by fast action, quick passing, and rapid swelling.

amateur: the unintentional status of many of the best American soccer players throughout their careers. This sad fact has resulted in extensive efforts by many groups to develop professional leagues with high salaries for these players. The Internal Revenue Service is underwriting their efforts.

ankle: noisiest joint in the body.

ankle wrap: elastic wrap designed to muffle ankle noises.

anterior cruciate: easily damaged ligament in the knee. Known for its ability to collect a variety of knee braces, and for being the primary reason every knee surgeon drives an expensive foreign car.

assistant coach: person on a team most likely to have a ball pump in his trunk, a ball bag in his garage, and no shower hooks in his bathroom.

athletic bag: mud-encrusted, moldy, smelly cloth bag used to store clean towels and antiseptic bandages.

avid: description of soccer fans, players, and coaches at the beginning of the season (see *disillusioned*).

b **back pass:** a pass to a teammate located to the rear of the passer, which usually results in the teammate kicking the ball into the rear of the passer.

balance: maintaining equilibrium between the desire to play soccer and the desire to have toenails that aren't black.

ball: highly pressurized mass of hot air surrounded by elastic bladder (see *coach*).

ball bag: large net-like contraption used to deliver soccer balls from car to playing field, and back again. These useful devices cannot be purchased separately; they are standard equipment on most station wagons.

banana kick: snappy dance step popular in Central America.

bicycle kick

bandages: absorbent cloth used primarily to soak up spilled water, juice, and heat rub in the bottom of equipment bags.

beg: the second most effective means of getting a favorable call from a referee (see *stock tips*).

bicycle kick: difficult maneuver performed by professional players to impress the fans, and by amateur players to break their tailbones.

bif: 1. missing the ball when kicking. 2. abbreviated form of the word bifocals, which are what coaches prescribe for players who *bif* too often.

boots: leather foot wrappings manufactured by a variety of companies, in all sizes and many styles, in an attempt to gain market share. Boots come in colorful boxes and are stored carefully by their proud owners in the closet for the first two weeks after purchase. Thereafter, they can only be found under the bed along with half-eaten sandwiches, in a soggy cardboard box in the garage, or encased in mud with petrified laces in the trunk of the car.

breakaway: other than a penalty kick, the only opportunity for an offensive player to go one-on-one with the opposing goalie. Breakaways usually result in one of three things: a. a goal; b. a save; or c. a cast.

bump: delicate maneuver requiring contact between players competing for the ball, with intention of gaining possession of the ball without gaining possession of a yellow card.

C callus: natural padding on bottom of the feet used to compensate for unnatural padding on the bottom of soccer boots (see *cleats*).

card

cap: item awarded to player selected for national team. There is no logical explanation why these highly skilled players were not provided with a traditional uniform.

captain: highly prized distinction usually awarded at the beginning of the game to the player most likely to start, least likely to get kicked out of the game, and who can still call the referee "Sir" or "Ma'am" after being viciously slide tackled for the fifth time by the 6′4″ defender on the other team.

card: what a player gets when committing a flagrant foul while in sight of the referee.

cast: hard plaster device usually applied to the leg. It serves as a convenient and conspicuous location for soccer graffiti. Several popular examples are; *Happiness Is Soccer, Ouch, Bicycle Kicks Are A Real Pain, Soccer Shoes For Rent, My Doctor Sent Me A Thank-You Post Card From Europe,* and *Soccer Really Cracks Me Up.*

catcall: "Here kitty!"

center circle: field marking whose primary function is to tell the grounds maintenance crew where to never place the rainbird sprinkler.

centermid: a a duplication duplication in in terms terms.

chalk: white powdery material used to line soccer fields and the inside of equipment bags.

chalkboard: instructional tool used by coaches to remind players of important things they've forgotten. Like where they should be standing, how they should be moving, and the location of the opposing team's goal.

cheers: bothersome sideline noise usually not directly associated with the action on the field.

chest trap: a poorly executed header.

chip shot: a shot by a kid named Chip.

clear: the weather condition most unlikely to occur during a soccer game.

cleats: rubber bumps on the bottom of soccer shoes which directly transmit shock of ground contact to the soles of the feet, regardless of the number of padded socks, shoe inserts, or bunion pads used.

coach: person who would be calling time-outs if they were legal.

coin toss: traditional ceremony preceding each game that determines which team will lose possession of the ball first.

cone: bright orange devices used in dribbling drills. Coaches like to place them in complex patterns and force their players to continuously dribble balls around them. Players like to have them placed in their coach's trunk and left there.

corner kick: a kicked ball which executes a 90 degree turn while in flight, usually with the assistance of the back of the head of a surprised teammate, opponent, or referee.

crossbar: metal or wood bar which holds the goalposts apart.

crossing pass: a long pass from one player to another which crosses the centerline of the field. This pass is most effective when the receiving player is open, which is usually not the case by the time the ball finally arrives.

crutches: signaling devices used by a player to notify the coach she would prefer to not be inserted into the game.

divot

dad: a common, but fairly ineffective, excuse for a youth soccer coach (see *mom*).

defender: a player whose primary function is to commit fouls outside the penalty box.

defense: the team most likely to score an own goal.

dig: the art of removing sod, dirt, and rocks from their normal resting place on the soccer field. This is usually accomplished unintentionally with the toe of the soccer boot, the knee cap, or the nose.

dim-witted: one of two conditions required to play, coach, or referee a soccer game (see *able-bodied*).

direct kick: anytime a player swings at and kicks the ball without hitting anything along the way, including other players, the ground, his other foot, or stray dogs which wandered onto the field.

disillusioned: description of soccer fans, players, and coaches at the end of the soccer season (see *avid*).

dissent: the act of conducting a highly passionate, brilliantly stated, and totally ineffective debate with the referee.

dive: a difficult maneuver used by enthusiastic players to make contact with the ball (which is a good idea) and the ground (which is not).

divot: 1. hole in ground left by a player after attempting a dive. 2. hole in forehead left by the ground after attempting a dive.

dmso: strong ointment which causes breath to smell like rotten oysters. Very effective in reducing pain, speeding up healing process, and eliminating social life.

draw: any game in which both teams scored the same number of goals. Due to unique nature of soccer, this only occurs under two circumstances; when both teams were evenly matched, or when they weren't.

drib: an abbreviated dribble, usually consisting of one touch of the ball and one collision with another player.

dribbler: player who successfully completes a dribble (see *ball hog*).

dribbling: what a player does to keep from passing.

"drop ball": verbal command given by the referee to a player who picks up the ball with his hands.

drop kick: a difficult kick used by goalies where the ball is allowed to hit the ground just prior to being kicked. This hard to control kick is used by international soccer goalies to move the ball rapidly to the far end of the field, and by youth soccer goalies to move themselves rapidly to the sidelines.

e **egg on:** the condition of a player sponsored by a local poultry farm shortly after scoring an own goal.

eighteen yard line: a line, beyond which most penalties are not committed, and inside of which most bad acting is performed.

ejection: player substitution called by the referee.

elbow: a sharp weapon employed by players to maintain their space and possession of the ball. When elbowing is used against a much shorter player it is called a clothesline. When elbowing is used against a much taller player it is called a referee's timeout.

end line: where the ball exits the playing surface after a missed shot, after a poorly

executed corner kick, and after an extremely poorly executed goal kick.

english: the spin placed on a kicked ball which alters its direction while in flight. Popular versions include: top spin, where the player kicks the top of the ball, thus causing it to drop faster than normal; side spin, where the player kicks the side of the ball, thus causing it to curve more than normal; and bottom spin, where the player kicks the bottom of the ball, thus causing it to go nowhere but the player goes to the hospital.

eye glasses: vision aids thought to be made obsolete on the soccer field by contact lenses and headers.

f

fake: a move with no follow-through.

faking an injury: what a player might be doing when he is rolling on the ground with his head buried in the grass and grasping his ankle. Referees can usually determine whether the player is faking by inspecting the condition of the ground on which the player is lying. Soft, green, and lush means he is faking. Wet, brown, and muddy means he should be removed from the field immediately.

fall: season of the year when more oranges are sliced, more water bottles are lost, and more soccer balls are bounced around in the trunk than any other time of the year.

falling: the act of slicing oranges, losing a water bottle, or placing a soccer ball in the trunk of the car.

fans: loving parents at youth soccer games, loving schoolmates at high school or college games, loving spouses at adult soccer games, and hateful youth, high school, college, and adult soccer players at professional soccer games.

fast: the desired speed you should kick balls in the direction of your opponents' goal.

fast break: the rapid movement of a team with the ball toward the opponent's goal with the intent of getting a shot off before the defense has a chance to get ready. Fast breaks are always followed by a weird wheezing sound coming from the referee.

faster: the undesired speed you should kick balls in the direction of your own goal.

fastest: the likely speed you will be substituted for after an own goal.

feint: move used by a player with the ball to fake a player without the ball into thinking she can become the player with the ball by moving to a place where the ball won't be.

final score: the statistical tabulation of the combined efforts of both teams, the impartiality of the referee, the eyesight of the linesmen, the level of enthusiasm of the fans, and the caliber of the groundskeeper.

first to the ball: 1. what coaches want their players to be, in order to gain possession of the ball and move it down the field. 2. what parents want their kids to be, so they can watch them touch the ball at least once during the game.

flail: the successful completion of the difficult "kick the air" maneuver. Usually followed by the *fall*, the *moan* and the *limp*.

foot: the many-boned appendage of the leg primarily responsible for the artful control of the soccer ball, maintaining balance while executing difficult maneuvers over uneven terrain, and keeping the laces tight on soccer boots.

football: a popular game in the United States where extremely large and strong

players wear extensive padding and helmets, and crash violently into each other. Not surprisingly, there are usually at least six referees assigned to each game.

forward: the direction a player is leaning just after being tripped, and just before hitting the ground.

fullback: a wide-bodied soccer player (see *halfback*).

g **game-ending whistle:** when play ends and excuses and bragging begin.

give-and-go: dribbling with a teammate's feet.

go: 1. verbal command given to teammates in an attempt to let them know when a through ball is about to be kicked and that they should prepare to advance quickly down the field to gain possession. 2. verbal command given to teammates in an attempt to get them out of the way.

goal: to play soccer forever.

goal box: area in which coaches love to have their goalkeeper use her hands, and hate to have the referee use her whistle.

goalie: player assigned important task of extending the life expectancy of the nets.

goalie gloves: gloves made from various rubberized materials designed to stick to the soccer ball in any weather condition except those in which the game is being played.

goalkeeper: person on the field most likely to know the score.

goal kick: a kick used by the defense after the other team has kicked the ball over the end line. This kick is designed to place the ball back in play, and the kicking team back on defense.

goal mouth: a goalie who likes to talk.

goalpost: posts located at both ends of a soccer field festooned with historic paraphernalia from past games, including hardened tape fragments, string with permanent knots, and rusted loops of wire. Although serving nicely as part of the framework for holding up the nets, these posts also serve as excellent places for goalies to place their used chewing gum, convenient places to lean against during boring parts of the game, and hard places to run into during the rest of the game.

goof: a slight miscue by a player which results in momentary embarrassment, but does not affect the outcome of the game. Typical *goofs* are: taking a header on the nose, missing a kick, tripping over your own shoelaces, dropping a ball during a throw-in, and telling the coach how to run a practice session. If committed more than once, *goofs* can often result in significant reductions in playing time.

groove: 1. the seams on a soccer ball where individual panels are sewn together. 2. the small indentations on soccer fields where knees are torn apart.

h

halfback: fullback after a successful diet (see *fullback*).

halftime: a forced period of rest between halves where players let their joints get stiff, their muscles get sore, and their ears get chewed off.

hammer: an indispensible tool used to pound stakes into the ground in order to stretch out the net. Hammers are usually found in the net bag when the ground is soft as butter, and in the locked trunk of the

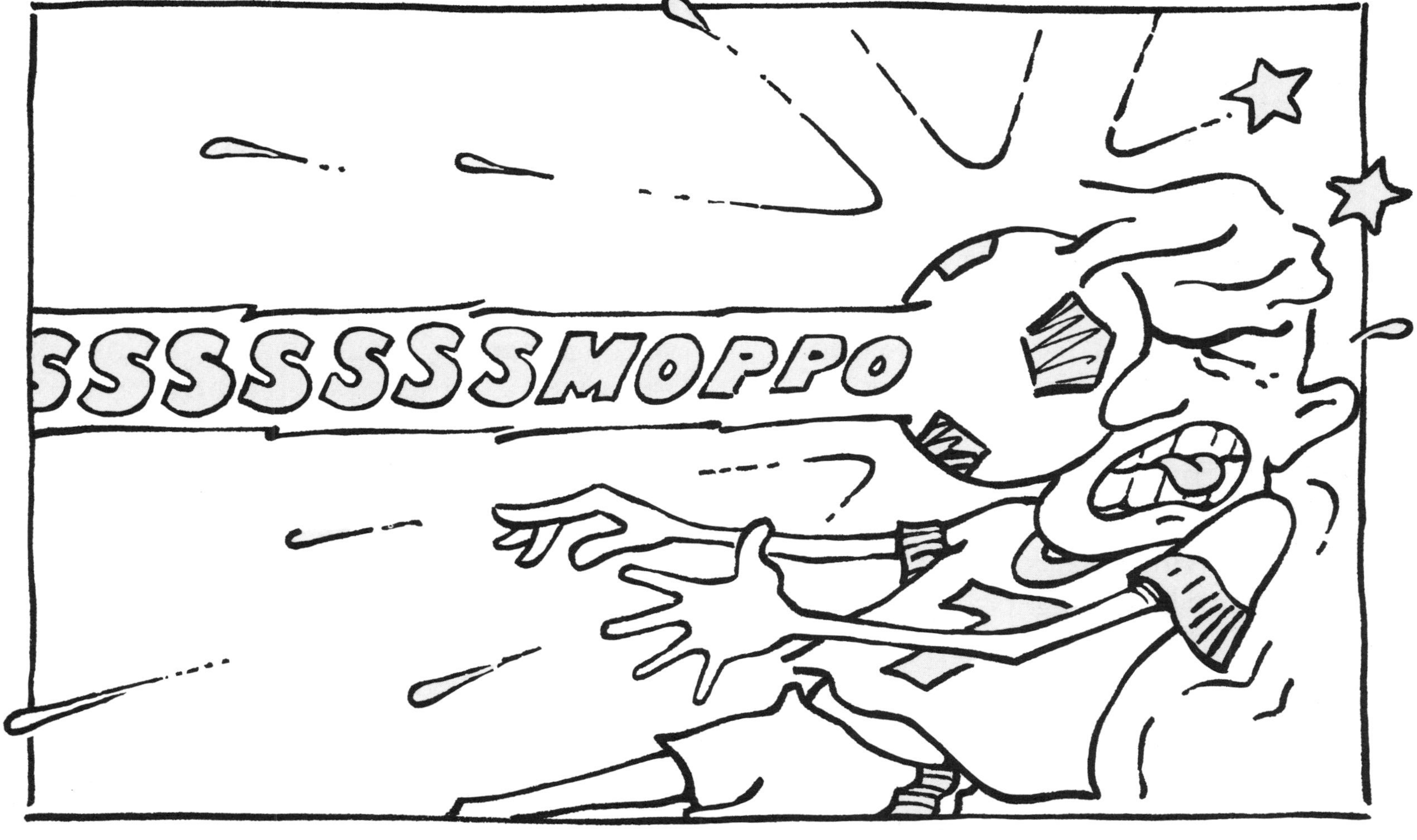
SSSSSSSSMOPPO

car in the parking lot a mile away when the ground is hard as concrete.

hand ball: 1. penalty called on a player for inadvertently allowing the ball to come in contact with his arm or hand. 2. penalty called on a player for inadvertently allowing referee see him purposely cause the ball to come in contact with his arm or hand.

hand-stitched: a technique used in the construction of high quality soccer balls and low quality soccer knees.

hat trick: the scoring of three goals by one player in one decade.

head: the part of the body used most in headers and least in fights.

header: hitting the ball with any part of the body above the neck; especially the ears, chin, and bridge of the nose.

heat rub: the secret ingredient in postgame pizzas.

heel: an important part of the foot responsible for keeping socks from bunching up around the toes.

heel tap: the intentional clipping of the heel of an opponent in an attempt to make up for the fact that he successfully got by you. The heel tap is thought to be an inappropriate tactic except when the opponent is likely to score or has just dribbled the ball through your legs.

hip check: a quick scan of the figures of the females on the sidelines by the males on the field, and vice versa.

hold on to her shirt: a common defensive strategy when slide tackles, heel taps, and land mines don't seem to work.

insignia

illegal tackle: tackling an opponent in such a manner as to cause her to lose possession of the ball, and her senses.

indirect kick: any kick which did not reach the intended destination.

indoor soccer: soccer games played in a variety of arenas such as old roller rinks, barns, field houses, and gymnasiums for the purpose of decreasing the effects of weather and increasing the effects of physical intimidation on the outcome of the game.

injury: a possible, and painful result of playing, watching, coaching, refereeing, or discussing soccer.

injury prone: a person who plays, watches, coaches, referees, or discusses soccer more than three times a week.

inside: a position on the field which is closer to the centerline than where the player is presently located. This is a good place to avoid due to the high incidence of bare ground, puddles, mud, and opponents.

insignia: the name and symbol of the sponsor, proudly displayed on soccer uniforms. On most teams, if asked, players could probably not give accurate directions to the sponsor's store, nor describe what is sold there.

intercept: removing the ball from an opponent's foot.

intercepted pass: a successful pass to the wrong player.

irate fan: standard issue for every soccer game. This person can usually be distinguished by his constant pacing of the sideline, mutterings about the ancestry of the referee and linesmen, and the megaphone hooked to his belt.

j

jeers: derisive comments made from the sidelines to remind players they are not alone.

jerk: the spectator on the sidelines most likely to have the loudest opinion and the least understanding of the game of soccer.

jersey: fancy name for moldy and badly stained shirt reserved for the newest and most junior member of the team.

j.o.g.: acronym for Jump Over Gila monsters, the first rule taught to new players in the Tucson Sunstroke Soccer League.

jolt: the transfer of a sizeable amount of force from an immovable object (ground, goal post, any defender weighing more than 200 pounds) to a movable object (you).

juggler: any parent trying to carry a water bottle, blanket, lawn chair, plastic container full of orange slices for halftime treats, medical kit, small ladder for installing nets, and corner flags from parking lot (usually located at least one quarter of a mile away) to the field. Official juggler status does not exist until at least one of the above items becomes loose and requires the assistance of a knee, foot, or forehead to keep from falling into the mud.

juggling: soccer solitaire.

juke: another form of faking, requiring more movement of the hips and upper legs than a feint. Usually not recommended for players weighing more than 280 pounds or 8 months pregnant.

jump: what a player does to avoid mud puddles, sprinkler heads, and serious injury.

jumping jacks: 1. warm-up exercise designed to loosen muscles and screw-in cleats. 2. one of many punishing exercises forced upon the players prior to the game to get them warm, loose, and irritable.

jump rope: a training device used by serious players to increase their foot speed, improve their endurance, develop their leg muscles, and acquire savage rope burns around the ankles and neck.

k **keeper:** any World Cup souvenir.

kick: the violent forward movement of the foot towards the ball. A kick can result in one of three conditions: a. contact is made with the ball, and the ball goes in the desired direction (see *direct kick*); b. contact is made with the ball, but the ball goes in the wrong direction (see *indirect kick*); and c. no contact is made with the ball (see *knee brace*).

kicker: the person who is kicking the ball. Not to be confused with the person kicking the ground (see *turf toe*), the person kicking the goalpost (see *foot fracture*), and the person kicking the referee (see *ejection*).

kickoff: the exciting ritual which begins each half and the embarrassing punishment which follows each score.

kids: those cute little creatures on the sidelines who play funny little games, sit on blankets, play with puppies and other small children, and somehow manage to get hit by every ball which goes out-of-bounds on their side of the field.

"kill it": the words that pass through a soccer player's mind just before he kicks the ball. Usually preceded by words like, "keep your head down," "take it easy," and "don't try to kill it," and almost always followed by, "argggghhh!"

kill it

k.i.s.s.: acronym for Kids in Soccer Saturday, the standard notation on calendars in many American homes on fall weekends.

kitchen sink: critical pregame warm-up device used to prepare oranges for consumption. Also a critical postgame device used to clean water bottles and bleach mud and blood out of socks and shin guards.

knee brace: an all-too-common treatment for soccer mania.

kneecap: a thick, flat, and triangular bone covering the anterior portion of the knee joint, and responsible for protecting it from injury (not very successfully), and banging into table legs at restaurants (very successfully).

laces: reliable fastening devices credited with 100% reliability except for the following circumstances: a. before the game (they break); b. during the game (they come untied); and c. at the end of the game (they turn into petrified knots which cannot be untied).

lame: something not quite right; like a leg, a kick, or a coach.

lame excuse: what a player needs from her doctor in order to be eligible to play after having been lame.

"leave it": command to another player on the same team when you don't have enough time to say, "You keep running as if you still had the ball, but leave it where it is and I will run by and initiate the dribble, hopefully placing the opposing team in a disadvantageous position, which will result in a probable shot, and if I don't mess up and the goalie does, a possible score. Okay?"

lucky bounce

l.e.e.r.: acronym for Let Exeter Eat Radishes, a popular team cheer used by the Cambridge School of Carrots.

limp: a method of walking used predominantly by players between the sidelines and their cars when girl/boy friends are present, or when they have just been outplayed by a kid half their size on the opposing team.

line: markings on field designed to provide evidence of exactly when the referee decides to run for his life.

linesman: referee-in-training.

loose: 1. the condition of teeth just after a header, and laces just before the kickoff. 2. the type of defensive coverage which gives the opposing team clear shots and coaches ulcers.

lose: the direct result of loose coverage by the defense.

loser: any team unlucky enough to have been scheduled to play an away game against a team with a multi-colored pennant on the sidelines, their name spray painted in the center circle, and a former World Cup player named Francois as their coach.

lucky bounce: the movement of the ball in a strange and unexpected direction as a result of hitting the ground, a player, the referee, or the goalpost. Lucky bounces are responsible for 18% of all completed passes, 42% of all goals, and 88% of all broken goalie noses.

lumpy field: a brutal field condition responsible for turned ankles, bad bounces, and fired groundskeepers.

lumpy player: an ugly player condition caused by playing on a lumpy field.

m **make a wall:** 1. a defensive maneuver designed to place as many players as possible into a position likely to cause them great bodily harm. 2. the soccer equivalent of playing dodge-ball with a cannon.

manager: for the smooth-running youth soccer team, there must be a person who is in touch with league officials, players, coaches, and parents, knows when the games start, has maps to all the fields, carries extra pairs of everything in the trunk, and isn't afraid to ask for money on a regular basis. Managers are usually either accountants, lawyers, longshoremen, or moms.

marker: pen used to write owner's name and phone number on a new soccer ball to reduce risk of loss. However, it is difficult to determine why this futile practice continues since such markings usually are worn off the ball within one week due to kicking, bouncing, and rolling. The world record for the longest time a player's name and number have stayed legible on a ball is three and one half weeks, not counting the time Danny "The Dirty" Douglas lost his ball under his bed for six months behind some dirty clothes, a half-eaten sandwich, and four pairs of outgrown soccer boots.

melon head: affectionate nickname for the player with the most own goals or headers during the season.

men's soccer: 1. version of soccer where skills and egos are unevenly matched. 2. version of soccer where the quality of play is directly proportional to the number of girlfriends on the sidelines.

midfield: area of field identified by the largest mud puddle, the deepest pool of stagnant water, or the barest patch of ground.

midfielder: player on field who is always trying to get back into position.

mom: indispensible member of any youth soccer team. She is responsible for keeping uniforms clean, getting players to practices on time, and knowing the difference between a throw-in and a slide trombone. Moms are usually the ones on the sidelines responsible for positive cheers for the kids on the field no matter how they are doing, and dirty looks at their husbands on the sidelines for acting like kids.

mud puddle: groundskeeper's way of getting back at soccer teams for leaving litter on the field.

n net: a ragged, loosely woven mesh affixed to the goalposts at both ends of the soccer field for the purpose of stopping balls that aren't stopped by the player responsible for stopping them.

net bag: magical device capable of transforming a brand new net into large, knotted masses of nylon, shower hooks, heavy wire, and straps of white tape. The only known method of reversing this process is to throw the knotted mass back into the bag, roll it around in the trunk for about six months, and then try again.

nostril: drain hole for poorly executed headers.

numerals: random set of numbers on the back of soccer uniforms. There is no known use for these numbers, except for referees to record when giving out yellow or red cards.

Needless to say, their elimination is being sought by various players' groups.

nutmeg: kicking the ball between the legs of an opponent; a difficult maneuver requiring the most advanced of skills, perfect timing, artful footwork, a keen eye, and an opponent with long legs.

O **obstruction:** the placing of one's body in a location which is likely to keep an opponent from reaching the ball, but not your throat.

offense: the team temporarily in possession of the ball.

offside: the side of the field furthest from the parking lot, rest rooms, or refreshment stand.

offside trap: what any team does to get the other team's spectators to have to stand on the offside.

orange slices: nutritional packages provided at halftime for players, in an attempt to pump them up for the second half, and to get rid of all those freezer-burned oranges forgotten for the past month in the back of the fruit drawer of the refrigerator.

orthopedic surgeon: soccer's equivalent of the twelfth man.

out-of-bounds: the location of a soccer ball just prior to a throw-in, or just after a poorly executed throw-in.

"over here": futile call to a teammate to notify him that you are open for a pass, but usually not heard until after the teammate is either surrounded, attacked, or prone.

over 30: a level of soccer play typified by a slightly slower pace and a slightly faster heart rate.

over 40: a level of soccer play typified by a significantly slower pace and a significantly faster heart rate.

over 50: a level of soccer play typified by no pace and no heart rate.

overtime: for players in good condition, a chance to extend their playing time. For players in bad condition, a chance to test their health benefits.

own goal: 1. any goal scored by the defense and claimed by the offense. 2. soccer's equivalent of striking out on one pitch.

parent: 1. large person on the sideline responsible for cheering at small person playing on the field and yelling at medium size person blowing whistle. 2. loving adults responsible for making sure youth players arrive at the right field (even if it is across town behind a small school they have never heard of, and which doesn't appear on any map), at the right time (usually at least 45 minutes before a game that will start 35 minutes late), with the right uniform (which is usually too big), and in the right state of mind (ready to stand on the sideline and be positive when their child only gets five minutes of playing time).

pass: an event preceded by, and immediately followed by, the touching of the ball by two players of the same team. A pass can take a fraction of a second to complete (when the receiver is standing a few meters away), or can take what seems like an eternity (when the receiver is standing wide-open in front of the opponent's goal).

pass it: what a player does to a soccer ball with his feet and to a head cold with his water bottle.

penalty: on-the-field spanking.

penalty kick: kicking an opponent on the shin.

pizza parlor: common location for postgame parties, probably due to the similarly round shape of a pizza and a soccer ball. Unfortunately, in some pizza parlors, the similarities do not stop there.

"play on!": typical call by referee who either did not see the foul, did not see which player fouled first, or did not remember the name of the foul he just saw.

Portland, Oregon: home of the Cool Change Cutups, the author's coed soccer team. Founded in 1986, this team has proven itself to be capable of reaching the highest level of soccer achievement; getting someone to pay for the shirts.

posterior cruciate: where the anterior cruciate ends up after a vicious slide tackle.

postgame party: where muscles get sorer, joints get stiffer, and excuses get bigger.

praise: the positive verbal feedback given to a player after scoring a goal, to a goalie after blocking a penalty kick, and to the coach after starting the son of the sponsor.

pregame pep talk: short meeting prior to game where important matters are discussed which are critical to the outcome of the game, but don't have anything to do with soccer.

professional soccer: only soccer game where there are more spectators than players.

prone: posture assumed by a goalie after a penalty kick, or by an offensive player after a penalizing kick.

puberty: the primary difference between U12 and U14 teams.

puddles: convenient devices on soccer fields used to clean boots, balls, and contact lenses.

q **quarrel:** an argument between players, parents, coaches, referees, linesmen, people walking their dogs, stray cats, or any combination of the above occurring within 50 yards of a soccer field.

quart: 1. amount of liquid consumed by a typical soccer player during a typical game during typical weather conditions. 2. amount of liquid sweated by a typical soccer player during a typical game during typical weather conditions. 3. amount of stomach acid produced by any soccer coach during any game during any weather condition.

question a call: a request by the coach to discuss a questionable call and the relative merits of eyeglasses with the referee.

quick feet: a scouting report term used to describe a soccer player with very short legs.

quiet: the undesirable condition of your sidelines after a goal has been scored.

r **rag:** the eventual fate of all kitchen towels.

red card: an embarrassed yellow card.

referee: black-clad individual responsible for deciding which infractions should be called, which should be ignored, and which should be rewarded.

rethrow: an embarrassing punishment for a player who somehow managed to miss the entire field on the first attempt.

round robin: 1. soccer tournament format where all teams have a chance to tie all other teams. 2. a red bird which has just swallowed a miniature soccer ball.

rugby: a derivative of soccer, but with bruises above the waist.

rules: the things that make the game of soccer safe and low scoring.

rush: the rapid movement of the entire forward line up the field in an attempt to gain an advantage and develop a chance for a shot. Usually results in either a shot, or a rush in the opposite direction.

sanitary socks: the gnarled, brownish, and smelly round mass in the bottom of most equipment bags.

scrimmage: a practice game, in which everything is the same as a real game, except the score, which is usually much higher and far more interesting.

shin guards: lumpy protective devices used to reduce, but not eliminate pain, discomfort, and scars as a result of being kicked. Usually they just deflect the force of the kick to an unprotected part of the leg like the foot, ankle, or knee cap.

shirts: 1. the team that gets to wear their heavy cotton jerseys during a scrimmage. This is usually the team you will be assigned to during scrimmages played on hot humid days at two in the afternoon. 2. the colorful garments worn by players to distinguish themselves from the other team, the referee, and anyone with any fashion sense.

shootout: five-minute event held after soccer game designed to determine what wasn't determined during the previous ninety minutes.

shorts: goal kicks which fail to reach the eighteen yard line.

shot: the sometimes intentional movement of the ball towards the sometimes intended goal.

shower hooks: curved metal contraptions used to attach nets to goalposts. These difficult-to-handle wire hoops are usually the only devices available for games played on days when you forgot your gloves and the temperature is below freezing with a 30 knot wind blowing off a nearby frozen lake.

shutout: common occurrence in soccer, which is directly responsible for the incredibly long life span of nets, and the short life span of goalies.

sidelines: the place where throw-ins are initiated, and ejections are terminated.

sidestep: difficult pregame warm-up drill intended to get players used to falling over.

skins: the team that does not get to keep their jerseys on during a scrimmage. This is usually the team you will be assigned to during scrimmages played on cold wet days at 8 in the morning the day after you got over a head cold.

sliced oranges: halftime treat provided for players to give them the necessary nutrients to go back out and get clobbered in the second half.

soccer: a game consisting of 22 skilled players, one impartial referee, two eagle-eyed linesmen, and one stupid ball.

soccer ball: a round object used by referees to entice players into committing fouls.

soccer field: usually rectangular, often lined, sometimes mowed, seldom seeded playing surface.

socks: fashionable elastic garments worn prominently on the lower extremities. Usually color-coordinated with the rest of the soccer ensemble, these distinctive items hug tightly to the ankles and calves giving a

slender and longer-legged look to the player while standing in front of the mirror at home. Unfortunately, they usually are transformed into soggy, flopping ankle weights draped heavily over the top of soccer boots after the first five minutes of the game.

spectators: people on sidelines responsible for making sure embarrassing maneuvers on the field are duly noted, and good plays are carefully ignored.

spin: the revolving motion a ball makes just after a kick, and the world makes just after a header.

sponge: mushy, absorbent pad used to dispense water from a bucket and 90% of the first aid to soccer players.

sponsors: companies with endless pictures of losing teams in their lobbies, usually with the owner's son or daughter in the front row.

"square": derogatory comment aimed at the guy playing soccer with black socks or a slide rule clipped to the band of his shorts.

steal: losing possession of a ball to an opponent without intent, assistance, or excuse.

stockings: socks, when still in the plastic bag.

stray dog: a required piece of equipment for every soccer field, these mangy, usually brown, and foul-smelling creatures are responsible for fertilizing the playing field just prior to the start of the game, making at least one mad dash across the field in pursuit of the ball, and slobbering on the face and cookie of a stroller-bound tot on the sidelines.

stretching

stress fracture: an injury recently discovered by orthopedic surgeons, which, if untreated, will result in more playing time and smaller medical bills.

stretching: painful method of warming up, usually avoided by players under twelve (because they don't need it), and over forty (because they don't want to risk serious injury before the game).

striker: offensive player responsible for mad dashes down the field, calling for the ball from wingers, and wearing out the nets (see *winger*).

substitution: what all players look forward to if they're on the sidelines, and dread if they're on the field.

sweat band: a group of overweight, overdressed, and overburdened marching musicians.

sweats: unattractive, baggy outergarment worn by soccer players to hide unattractive, baggy soccer uniforms.

sweeper: key defensive position usually filled by the player on the team with the quickest feet and the thickest shin guards.

switch: passing the ball to the only player on the same team who didn't expect it.

tackle: separating the ball from the player, and the player from the vertical plane.

taking a dive: the strategic throwing of one's body to the ground with the intent of drawing a foul. This maneuver is best performed on soft portions of the field with the intent of not drawing blood.

talent: what differentiates one player from another; besides size, weight, strength, endurance, skill, selection of proper boots for

throw-in

URK

the field conditions, amount of sleep the night before, length of time since last big meal, amount of sugar in system, time of day, weather conditions, field conditions, hoarseness of coach, quality of other team, attendance of girl/boy friend, eyesight, parentage, likelihood of shoelaces becoming untied, freshness of orange slices at halftime, location of nearest portable toilet, how favorite professional team did the day before, proximity of next big test, score on last big test, social life, self confidence, and whether socks will keep falling down or not.

teammate: 1. any player on the field with the same color uniform, but not necessarily the same intentions. 2. another person you have to dribble around.

t.g.i.f.: acronym for Toes Go In First, instructions imprinted on the inside of the soccer boots of all players in the U16 IQ league.

thigh trap: a poorly executed chest trap.

"through": call to another player on your team indicating you are about to pass due to exhaustion or fast approaching defender.

through pass: a pass to the opposing goalie which you hope will be intercepted by your own forwards.

throw-in: difficult method of returning a ball to play, intentionally designed to remind players how much easier it is to use their feet.

tie game: the normal condition at the beginning and end of most soccer games.

toe: 1. pain center of the foot. 2. useless appendage attached conspicuously to the front of the foot in order to increase the likelihood of kicking the ball the wrong way and tripping.

toenail: blackened and splintered fragment found clinging to the inside of the sock after a soccer game.

toe touches: terrible exercise used by coaches to build their players' conditioning, toe-eye coordination, leg strength, and use of foul language.

tongue: the flap under the laces of soccer boots which covers and protects the only portion of the foot susceptible to injury other than the ankle, big toe, big toe nail, ball, small toe, heel, achilles tendon, arch, instep, outstep, third toe, the small webbing between each of the toes, the second biggest toe, the other nails, the fourth toe, and the small balls of fuzz between the toes.

tournament: the fastest way to ruin a perfectly good soccer field.

towel: a fluffy white thing used at home in kitchens and bathrooms. These are not to be confused with the gnarly grey things used at soccer games (see *rag*).

trap: the art of stopping the ball with some part of the anatomy while avoiding serious injury, embarrassment, deep muscle bruises, or losing the ability to understand abstract thoughts.

triangle: a formation where three offensive players place themselves in a triangular pattern. This enables them to increase their chance of having an open pass, confusing the opposing team, and not running into each other.

trip: removing the equilibrium from an opposing player, without her permission.

trophy: plastic, wood, and metal sculpture awarded for a team's blood, sweat, and tears.

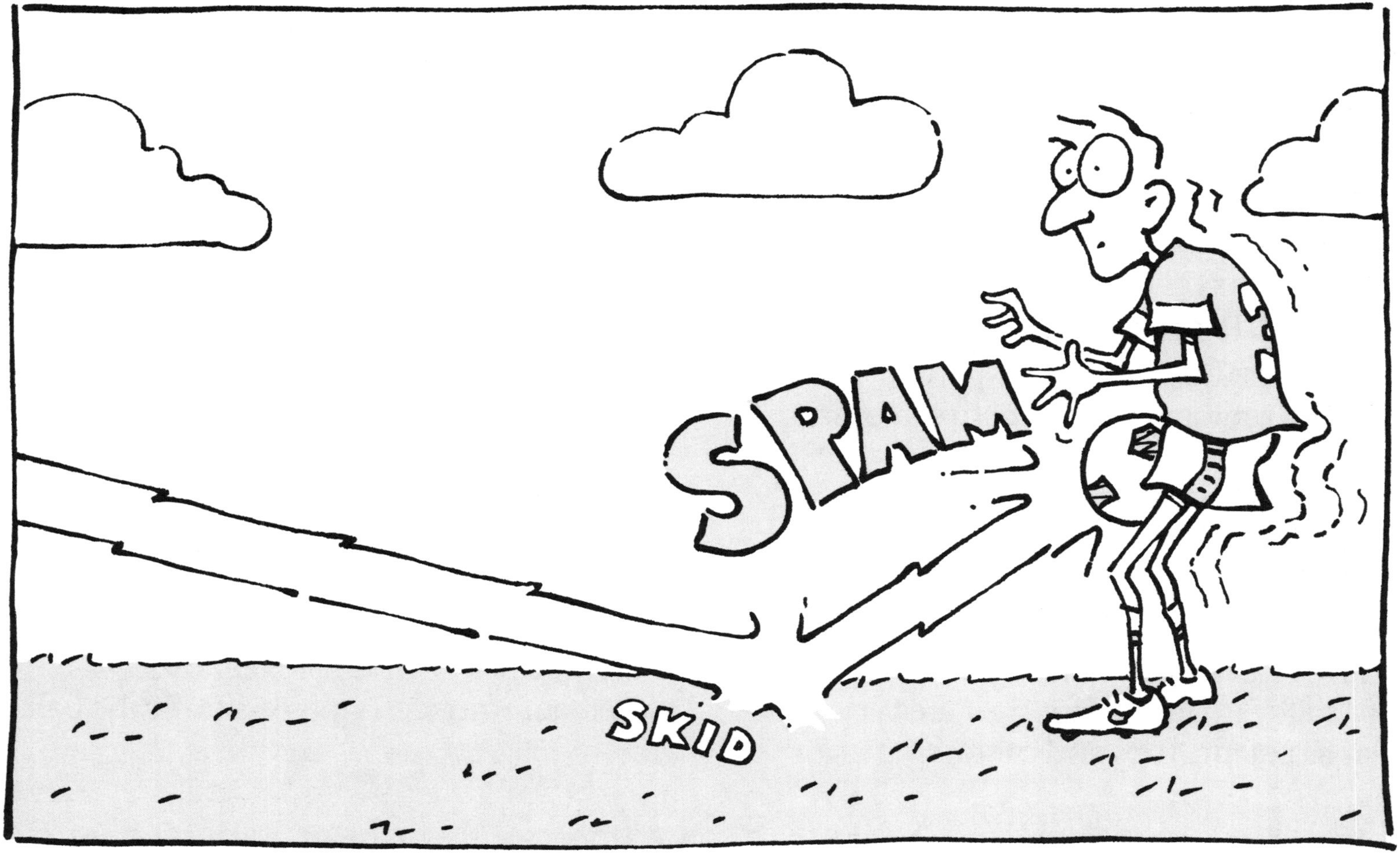
SPAM
SKID

tupperware: the largest American manufacturer of soccer equipment (see *orange slices*).

turf: soft, greenish, lush organic substance found surrounding soccer fields.

turf shoes: soccer shoes featuring many small cleats on the bottom, and even more cleat marks on the top.

Uunderwear: only part of the soccer uniform washed between every practice and every game.

uniforms: inexpensive set of clothing, usually garishly colored, and featuring the name and logo of a retired soccer player's company. Not surprisingly, soccer uniforms have not obtained the popularity of tennis or rugby uniforms, but they are very popular as pajama tops and car buffing rags.

unintentionally: 1. the method by which most adults take up playing soccer. 2. the method by which most parents take up coaching soccer. 3. the method by which most referees take up refereeing soccer. 4. the method by which most spectators compliment referees and coaches of soccer teams.

unlucky: good excuse for a bad play.

upfield: a place on the soccer field accessible only by running, and which usually shifts to another, distant location just before you get there.

Vvain: what a player is called who manages to keep his socks up during the entire contest.

victim: a player who has recently lost a wallet, automobile, or possession of the ball.

vain

victory: ending the game with at least one more goal, one less red card, or one less serious injury than the opposing team.

virgin ball: a soccer ball which has not spent a winter in the trunk of the car along with tire chains, ball pump, umbrellas, a lose tire iron, three heavy metal tools, and one full lunch bag from October.

Wall defense: the construction of an impenetrable barrier in front of the net, which usually does not succeed in blocking the ball but does block the goalie's vision.

warm-up: pregame exercises designed to remove last week's mud from the bottom of soccer boots.

watches: the timepieces worn on both wrists of many referees to keep track of elapsed time during a soccer game. The watch on the right wrist is used as the primary timepiece, the watch on the left wrist is used as the secondary timepiece, and the clock on the bank across the street is used as the official timepiece.

water bottle: container used to transport liquids from the sink at home (where it is filled), to the trunk of the car (where it is forgotten), and back to the sink at home (where it is emptied until the next soccer game).

whiff: any kick which results in the foot coming in contact with air not surrounded by a rubber or leather bladder.

whistle: 1. device used by referee to pretend she has control of play. 2. device used by referee in rating the acting performances of soccer players on the field.

wicked bounce: despite being perfectly round, a soccer ball can bounce in unpre-

winter soccer

dictable directions at the worst possible time, with the greatest possible negative effect, and usually when there are at least three camcorders covering the event on the sidelines.

winger: offensive player responsible for mad dashes down the field, centering the ball to teammate playing striker, and retrieving ball from playful German shephards on the sidelines (see *striker*).

winter soccer: soccer typified by ten-second halftimes.

women's soccer: version of soccer where the quality of play is directly proportional to the number of boyfriends on the sidelines.

X **xray:** soccer's equivalent of team photos.

Y **yard:** place where soccer is practiced, and mowing is avoided.

yawn: to open the mouth wide, in an involuntary reaction to fatigue or boredom. A yawn is usually preceded by a visit from your third cousin, a two-hour lecture on vanilla pudding, or a scoreless first half.

yelling: the sounds which emanate from the sidelines, waft uselessly across the field, and then land effectively and clearly on the opposite side of the field.

yellow card: referee's business card.

yesterday: the day you should have been practicing your team's defense against direct kicks.

youth soccer: any soccer game whose participants are as young as they act (see *adult soccer*).

Z **zigzag:** moving in an unpredictable manner to confuse your opponent and to make your coach think you know what you are doing.

zing: the resonant sound a soccer goalpost makes when hit solidly by a well hit soccer ball or a well pushed soccer player.

zip: rapid movement of a player, usually in the direction of the portable toilet.

zone defense: assigning specific areas for defensive players to guard, regardless of the location of the opponents, the location of the ball, or the outcome of the game.

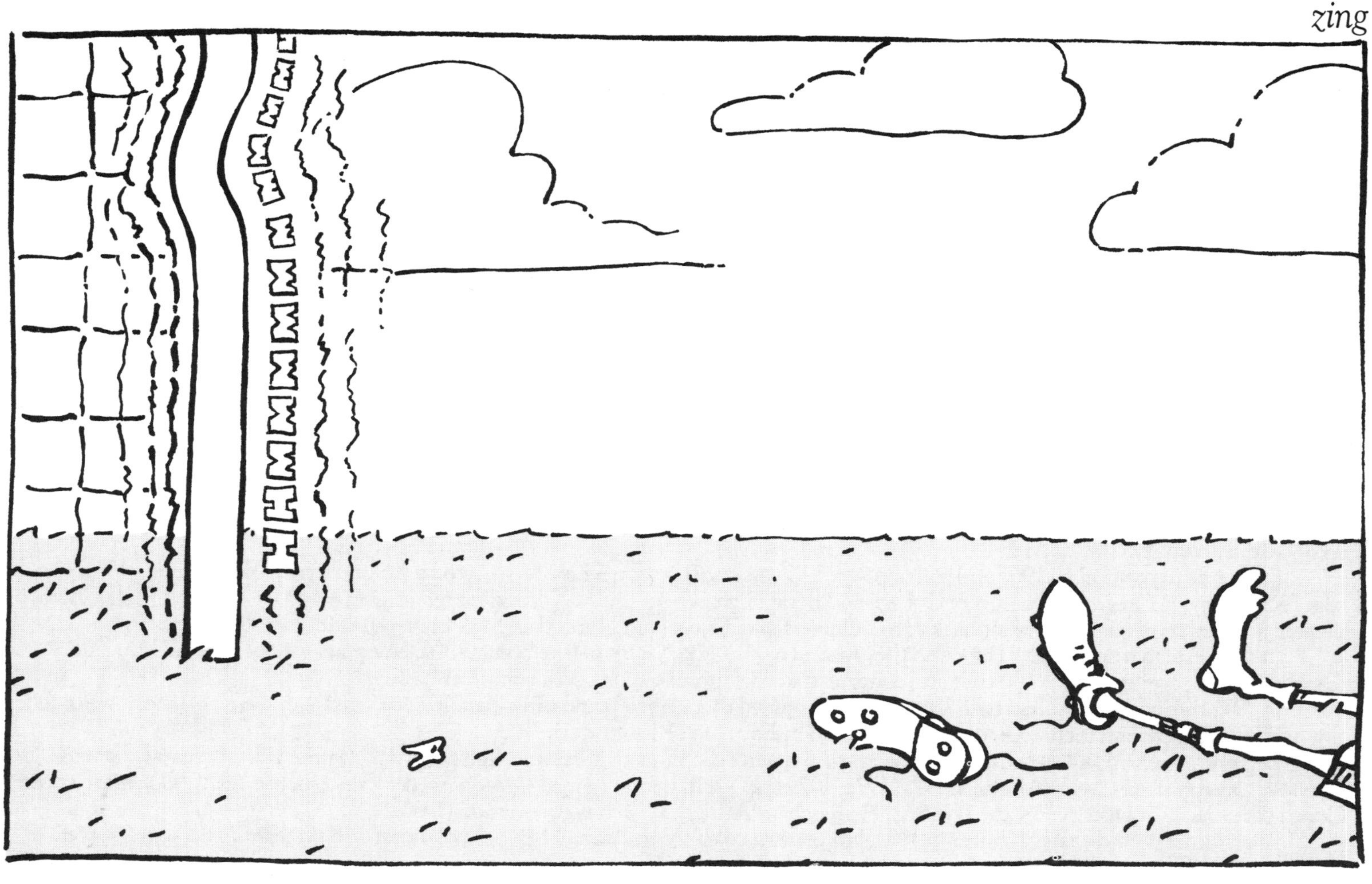
zing

PETER EVAN SMITH
1934-1986

This book is dedicated to the memory of Peter Evan Smith, a man who dedicated his life to the physical and emotional development of young people.

Pete was born in New Zealand on August 26, 1934, and was an outstanding rugby and track athlete. In 1956 he was national champion in the 440 yard dash and runner-up in the 220. He also qualified for the New Zealand Olympic Team that year, but was unable to compete due to injury.

Pete came to the U.S. in 1960 and attended the University of Oregon where he received a B.S. in Physical Education in 1961. He coached at Central Oregon Community College and Bend High School until 1970, and his teams won many District and State Championships. During this time Pete went back to the University of Oregon and earned an M.S. in Physical Education in 1968.

In 1970 Pete married Cheryl Petty and they moved to Portland, Oregon. Pete became an elementary school Physical Education teacher in the Beaverton School District and continued to coach youth sports on a volunteer basis.

In 1971 Pete and Cheryl had twin daughters and named them Kirsten and Gretchen. It is rumored they were both born wearing track shoes, and Pete had them race to see which would be born first. Kirsten won.

Beginning in 1975 Pete became the coach of the women's soccer team at Aloha High School. Over the next six years his teams won four Oregon State Championships (1977, 1978, 1979 and 1981), he was named Oregon Soccer Coach of the Year (1980), and Soccer Coach of the Year for District 7 by the National High School Athletic Coaches Association (1980).

Pete was diagnosed to have cancer in 1984, but continued to coach Aloha High School soccer and ski teams, and youth soccer teams. He died on January 3, 1986 and we miss him very much.